chicken creative

chicken creative

Published by:
TRIDENT PRESS INTERNATIONAL
801 12th Avenue South, Suite 400
Naples, Fl 34102 USA
Tel: + 1 239 649 7077
Email: tridentpress@worldnet.att.net
Websites: www.trident-international.com
          www.chefexpressinternational.com

Creative Chicken
© Trident Press International

Publisher
Simon St. John Bailey

Editor-in-chief
Isabel Toyos

Includes Index
ISBN 1582797668
UPC 6 15269 97668 5

2004 Edition
Printed in Colombia by Cargraphics S.A.

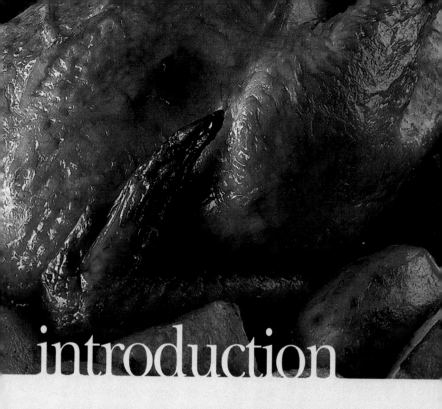

introduction

Chicken appeared as an invaluable meal on the tables of ancient Egypt, Greece, Rome and Asia. Today, almost all global cuisines use it one way or another; this is why we have inherited recipes from such diverse origins as Japanese teriyaki, Moroccan wings, or French Coq au Vin, just to name the most popular.

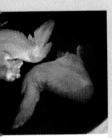

Goes with everything

Far from imposing, its delicate flavor combines well with all side dishes and condiments. Pan-fried with potatoes, in salads with avocado or grilled with lemon, chicken always plays the leading role in meals.

Nutritional values and assets

Rich in protein, essential aminoacids, A and B vitamins, and minerals like iron and zinc, it is easily digested. Range chickens are highly recommended since their meat, superior in flavor and texture, is less fatty, more natural and healthier.

The best choice

The skin of fresh chicken should have an all over yellowish aspect, without bruises, torn parts or excessive moisture. The flesh must be firm, compact and slightly pink colored. When buying frozen chicken make sure the package is intact and no ice has formed, a sign cold storage was interrupted.

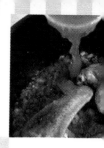

How to preserve

Fresh chicken can be stored up to three days
in the coolest part of the refrigerator (about
4°C/8°F). When bought frozen, it must be
placed immediately in the freezer. It's better
to use ground chicken immediately. Once
cooked it can be frozen up to six months.

Chicken pieces

- Individual pieces (for stews and casseroles)
- Whole breasts (for barbecues or oven grilled)
- Boneless breasts (for pan-frying)
- Drumsticks (breaded and fried)
- Ground (for hamburgers, terrines or fillings)
- Strips (for oriental stir-fries)
- Wings (for crunchy snacks)
- Boneless thighs (for filling)

With or without skin?

For certain recipes, or when cooking low fat
meals, chicken skin must be removed. Leave
it on when cooking chicken in salt, spit
roaster, or by the typical Argentine country
technique consisting in covering chicken with
fragrant herbs and wet clay before roasting.
For famous French dish poularde demi deuil,
with truffle slices stuffed under the skin, or
when making slow cooking stews and
casseroles, skin must also be left on.

Difficulty scale

■☐☐I Easy to do

■■☐I Requires attention

■■■I Requires experience

chicken
and corn chowder

■□□ | Cooking time: 21 minutes - Preparation time: 25 minutes

ingredients

> 1 tablespoon vegetable oil
> 1 small onion, diced
> 250 g/8 oz boneless chicken breast fillets, shredded
> 3 potatoes, chopped
> 3¹/2 cups/875 ml/1¹/2 pt chicken stock
> 315 g/10 oz canned sweet corn kernels, drained and coarsely chopped
> 1¹/4 cups/315 ml/ 10 fl oz milk
> 1 bay leaf
> freshly ground black pepper
> 1 tablespoon lemon juice
> 2 tablespoons chopped fresh parsley
> 1 tablespoon snipped fresh chives
> 60 g/2 oz grated Parmesan cheese

method

1. Heat oil in a saucepan over a medium heat, add onion and cook, stirring, for 4-5 minutes or until onion is soft. Add chicken and cook for 2 minutes longer or until chicken just changes color.

2. Add potatoes and stock and bring to the boil. Reduce heat and simmer for 10 minutes or until potatoes are almost cooked. Stir sweet corn, milk, bay leaf and black pepper to taste into stock mixture and bring to the boil. Reduce heat and simmer for 3-4 minutes or until potatoes are cooked. Remove bay leaf. Stir in lemon juice, parsley, chives and black pepper to taste. Just prior to serving, sprinkle with Parmesan cheese.

....
Serves 6

tip from the chef

To chop sweet corn, place in a food processor or blender and process using the pulse button until coarsely chopped. Creamed sweet corn can be used in place of the kernels if you wish. If using creamed sweet corn there is no need to chop it.

warm spicy
chicken green salad

■■□ | Cooking time: 10 minutes - Preparation time: 30 minutes

method

1. Melt butter in a frying pan over a high heat and stir-fry chicken on both sides. Season with salt, pour in balsamic vinegar and cook till reduced. Stand.

2. To make dressing, combine honey with vinegar and salt in a bowl, whisk to combine. Add chives, peach and half of the chilies, add oil beating until smooth.

3. On a serving platter make a bed with rocket, endive and lettuce. Place chicken and snow peas on top. Drizzle with dressing and garnish with remaining chilies.

Serves 4

ingredients

> 60 g/2 oz butter
> 4 boneless chicken breasts fillets, cooked and sliced
> salt
> 1/4 cup balsamic vinegar
> 200 g/7 oz snow peas, cooked
> rocket, curly endives and lettuce leaves, washed and drained

hot dressing

> 1 tablespoon honey
> 1/8 cup balsamic vinegar
> 1 teaspoon salt
> 2 tablespoons snipped chives
> 1 peach, stoned, peeled and finely chopped
> 4 fresh chilies, diagonally sliced
> 1/2 cup olive oil

tip from the chef

This salad can be served in winter as well as summer. Makes for a perfect starter or as a main dish, depending on the occasion.

chicken
and mango pasta salad

■ ☐ ☐ | Cooking time: 8-10 minutes - Preparation time: 10 minutes

method

1. Cook pasta in boiling water in a large saucepan following packet directions. Drain, rinse under cold running water and drain again.
2. Place pasta, chicken, water chestnuts and mangoes in a bowl and toss to combine.
3. To make dressing, place mayonnaise, chutney, spring onions, coriander and black pepper to taste in a bowl and mix to combine. Spoon dressing over salad and toss to combine. Cover and chill until required.

Serves 6

ingredients

> **500 g/1 lb large shell pasta**
> **1 cooked chicken, flesh cut into bite-sized pieces**
> **220 g/7 oz canned water chestnuts, drained and sliced**
> **440 g/14 oz canned mangoes, drained and sliced**

mango chutney dressing

> **1 cup/250 g/8 oz low-oil mayonnaise**
> **1/2 cup/155 g/5 oz sweet mango chutney**
> **2 spring onions, finely chopped**
> **2 tablespoons chopped fresh coriander**
> **freshly ground black pepper**

tip from the chef

Chicken salads are a great addition to a buffet or one such as this is a substantial one-dish meal. Leftover cooked turkey is a tasty alternative to chicken and when fresh mangoes are in season use these rather than canned ones.

chicken
waldorf loaf

■□□ | Cooking time: 0 minutes - Preparation time: 30 minutes

ingredients

> 1 cottage loaf
> 1 Granny Smith apple, finely chopped
> 60 g/2 oz walnuts, chopped
> 3 spring onions, finely chopped
> 2 tablespoons chopped fresh parsley
> 1/2 cup/125 g/4 oz mayonnaise
> freshly ground black pepper
> 10 spinach leaves, stalks removed
> 3 boneless chicken breast fillets, cooked and sliced
> 4 tomatoes, sliced

method

1. Cut top off the loaf and scoop out middle, so that only the crust remains as a large bread case. Reserve top of loaf. The crumbs from the center will not be used in this recipe, but can be made into bread crumbs.

2. Place apple, walnuts, spring onions, parsley, mayonnaise and black pepper to taste in a bowl and mix to combine. Place a layer of spinach leaves in base of bread case, top with a layer of chicken, a layer of apple mixture and finally a layer of tomato slices. Repeat layers, ending with a layer of spinach, until all ingredients are used and loaf is filled. Replace top and wrap loaf in aluminum foil. Place a board on top of loaf, weight down and refrigerate overnight. Serve cut into wedges.

....
Serves 8

tip from the chef

This can also be a perfect picnic dish – delicate chicken breasts are combined with Waldorf salad ingredients, placed in a bread case, wrapped in aluminum foil and refrigerated overnight. All you have to do in the morning is pack the picnic basket and you are ready to go.

chicken
avocado strudel

■ □ □ I Cooking time: 35 minutes - Preparation time: 25 minutes

method

1. To make filling, heat oil in a frying pan and cook onion and curry powder for 4-5 minutes or until onion is soft. Transfer onion mixture to a bowl, add cream cheese, chicken, red pepper, mushrooms, avocado and black pepper to taste. Mix well to combine.

2. Layer filo pastry sheets on top of each other, brushing between layers with oil. Top pastry with chicken mixture and roll up tightly, tucking ends under. Place on a baking tray, brush with oil, sprinkle with sesame seeds and bake at 180°C/350°F/Gas 4 for 30 minutes or until golden.

....

Serves 6

ingredients

> 10 sheets filo pastry
> 4 tablespoons vegetable oil
> 2 tablespoons sesame seeds

chicken avocado filling

> 1 tablespoon oil
> 1 small onion, chopped
> 2 teaspoons curry powder
> 200 g/6 1/2 oz cream cheese, softened
> 2 chicken breast fillets, cooked and cut into strips
> 1/2 red pepper, sliced
> 8 button mushrooms, sliced
> 1 avocado, stoned, peeled and sliced
> freshly ground black pepper

tip from the chef

For a lower calorie version, ricotta cheese can be used instead of cream cheese.

italian
chicken in a pan

■☐☐ I Cooking time: 15 minutes - Preparation time: 15 minutes

ingredients

> 6 boneless chicken breast fillets, skinned
> seasoned flour
> 1 egg, beaten
> dried breadcrumbs
> ¼ cup/60 ml/2 fl oz vegetable oil
> 500 g/1 lb bottled tomato pasta sauce
> 6 slices prosciutto or ham
> 6 slices mozzarella cheese
> 6 sprigs fresh sage

tip from the chef

In this recipe, fresh sliced tomatoes placed under the mozzarella sheets can be used instead of the bottled tomato sauce.

method

1. Place chicken between sheets of greaseproof paper and pound lightly to flatten. Dust with flour, then dip in egg and finally coat with breadcrumbs (a). Place on a plate lined with plastic food wrap and refrigerate for 15 minutes.

2. Heat oil in a large frying pan over a medium heat, add chicken and cook for 2-3 minutes each side (b) or until golden. Remove from pan and set aside.

3. Add pasta sauce to pan and cook over a medium heat, stirring, for 4-5 minutes or until hot. Place chicken in a single layer on top of sauce, then top each fillet with a slice of prosciutto or ham, a slice of cheese (c) and a sprig of sage. Cover and simmer for 5 minutes or until chicken is cooked through and cheese melts. Serve immediately.

....
Serves 6

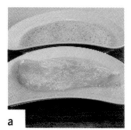
a

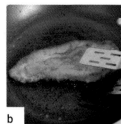
b

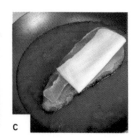
c

chicken
with oregano and lemon

■□□ | Cooking time: 25 minutes - Preparation time: 20 minutes

method

1. Season chicken with dried oregano, pepper and salt.
2. Heat oil in a large fry pan.
3. Add chicken, potatoes and onions, and brown quickly for 2-3 minutes.
4. Pour in stock, cover, and simmer for 10-15 minutes or until chicken is cooked.
5. Add lemon juice and fresh oregano. Season to taste. Cook for 3 minutes longer. Serve immediately.

....

Serves 4

ingredients

> 4 chicken breasts
> 2 teaspoons dried oregano
> freshly ground pepper and salt
> 2 tablespoons olive oil
> 600 g/20 oz potatoes, sliced to 5 mm/$^1/_5$ in
> 1 bunch spring onions, trimmed and halved
> 125 ml/4 fl oz chicken stock
> 75 ml/2$^1/_2$ fl oz lemon juice
> 2 sprigs oregano, chopped

tip from the chef

This recipe is delicious when fresh herbs are used. It's always good to have a plant, even if it is on a window box in the kitchen.

vineyard
chicken

■ ■ □ | Cooking time: 35 minutes - Preparation time: 30 minutes

ingredients

- > **4 boneless chicken breast or thigh fillets**
- > **2 teaspoons vegetable oil**
- > **2 onions, sliced**
- > **2 cloves garlic, crushed**
- > **440 g/14 oz canned tomatoes, undrained and mashed**
- > **1 green pepper, chopped**
- > **1 cup/250 ml/4 fl oz dry white wine**

ricotta filling

- > **125 g/4 oz ricotta cheese, drained**
- > **2 tablespoons chopped fresh basil**
- > **freshly ground black pepper**

method

1. Make a deep slit in the side of each chicken fillet to form a pocket.
2. To make filling, place ricotta cheese, basil and black pepper to taste in a bowl and mix to combine. Fill pockets with filling (a) and secure with toothpicks.
3. Heat oil in a large frying pan, add onions and garlic and cook, stirring, for 3 minutes or until onions are soft. Add tomatoes (b), green pepper and wine (c) to pan and cook, stirring, for 2 minutes.
4. Add chicken to pan (d), cover and simmer, turning chicken occasionally, for 30 minutes or until chicken is tender.

....
Serves 4

tip from the chef

This recipe can be completed to the end of step 2 several hours in advance.

a

b

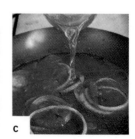

c

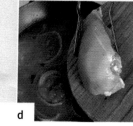

d

coq au vin

■ ■ □ | Cooking time: 100 minutes - Preparation time: 10 minutes

method

1. Toss chicken in flour to coat. Shake off excess flour and set aside.
2. Heat oil in a large, nonstick frying pan over a medium heat and cook chicken in batches, turning frequently, for 10 minutes or until brown on all sides. Remove chicken from pan and drain on absorbent kitchen paper.
3. Add garlic, onions or shallots and bacon to pan and cook, stirring, for 5 minutes or until onions are golden. Return chicken to pan, stir in stock and wine and bring to the boil. Reduce heat, cover and simmer, stirring occasionally, for 1¹/₄ hours or until chicken in tender. Add mushrooms and black pepper to taste and cook for 10 minutes longer.

ingredients

> 2 kg/4 lb chicken pieces
> ¹/₂ cup/60 g/2 oz seasoned flour
> 2 tablespoons olive oil
> 2 cloves garlic, crushed
> 12 pickling onions or shallots, peeled
> 8 rashers bacon, chopped
> 1 cup/250 ml/8 fl oz chicken stock
> 3 cups/750 ml/1¹/₄ pt red wine
> 250 g/8 oz button mushrooms
> freshly ground black pepper

Serves 6

tip from the chef

Wine is a natural flavor essential for the meat. For that reason, only good quality wines should be used in this and all recipes.

chicken
wings moroccan style

■■□ | Cooking time: 55 minutes - Preparation time: 15 minutes

ingredients

> 2 tablespoons oil
> 1 kg/2 lb tray chicken wings
> 1 large onion, finely chopped
> 1 clove garlic, crushed
> 1 1/2 teaspoons chopped fresh ginger
> 1/2 teaspoon ground turmeric
> 1/2 teaspoon cumin
> 1/2 cinnamon stick
> 1/4 cup/60 ml/2 fl oz cider vinegar
> 450 g/15 oz canned apricot nectar
> salt, pepper
> 100 g/3 oz dried prunes, pitted
> 100 g/3 oz dried apricots
> 1 tablespoon honey
> 1/4 cup/60 ml/2 fl oz lemon juice
> steamed couscous or rice to serve

method

1. Heat oil in a wide-based saucepan or lidded skillet, add chicken wings a few at a time (a) and brown lightly on both sides. Remove to a plate as they brown.
2. Add onions and fry for 2 minutes (b). Stir in garlic, ginger and spices. Cook while stirring for 1 minute, return chicken to the pan, stir and turn the wings to coat with spices. Add vinegar and apricot nectar (c), season to taste. Cover and simmer for 25 minutes.
3. Add prunes, apricots, honey and lemon juice (d). Cover and simmer 10 minutes and then remove lid and simmer uncovered for 5 minutes. If a thicker sauce is desired, remove wings and fruit to a serving platter, increase heat and boil until sauce reduces and thickens, stirring occasionally. Pour sauce over wings. Serve immediately with steamed couscous or rice.

....
Serves 3-4

tip from the chef

For a more substantial meal, replace the chicken wings for drumsticks.

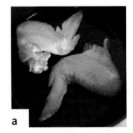

a

chicken
and pimento casserole

■ ■ □ | Cooking time: 23 minutes - Preparation time: 22 minutes

method

1. Heat oil in a large frying pan and cook chicken, stirring, over a medium heat for 2-3 minutes (a) or until chicken just changes color. Remove chicken from pan and set aside.

2. Add turnip, onions and pimentos to frying pan and cook for 3-4 minutes. Stir in wine (b) and tomatoes and bring to the boil, stirring, over a medium heat, then reduce heat and simmer, uncovered, for 10 minutes or until turnip is tender. Return chicken to pan and cook for 3-4 minutes longer (c) or until chicken is cooked. Stir in basil and serve immediately.

....
Serves 4

ingredients

> **2 tablespoons vegetable oil**
> **4 boneless chicken breast fillets, cut into strips**
> **1 turnip, cut into strips**
> **2 onions, chopped**
> **440 g/14 oz canned pimentos, drained and cut into strips**
> **1 cup/250 ml/8 fl oz dry white wine**
> **440 g/14 oz canned tomatoes, undrained and mashed**
> **3 tablespoons chopped fresh basil**

tip from the chef

All this easy chicken dish needs to make a complete meal is hot garlic bread or crusty bread rolls and a salad of mixed lettuce and herbs.

a

b

c

smoked
chicken

■□□ | Cooking time: 80 minutes - Preparation time: 5 minutes

ingredients
> **¹/2 cup/125 g/4 oz sugar**
> **3 tablespoons tea leaves**
> **2 tablespoons salt**
> **1 x 1.5 kg/3 lb chicken**
> **freshly ground black pepper**
> **1 tablespoon soy sauce**
> **2 teaspoons sesame oil**

method
1. Line a baking dish with sheets of aluminum foil large enough to completely enclose the chicken. Combine sugar, tea leaves and salt and spread out over foil. Place a roasting rack in the baking dish and place chicken on rack. Sprinkle chicken liberally with black pepper, bring foil up around chicken to completely enclose and bake at 190°C/375°F/Gas 5 for 1 hour.
2. Combine soy sauce and sesame oil. Open foil parcel, brush chicken with soy sauce mixture and bake, uncovered, for 20 minutes longer or until chicken is cooked through. To serve, cut into pieces and serve immediately.

Serves 6

tip from the chef
Chicken cooked in this way is moist with a crisp skin and distinctive flavor.

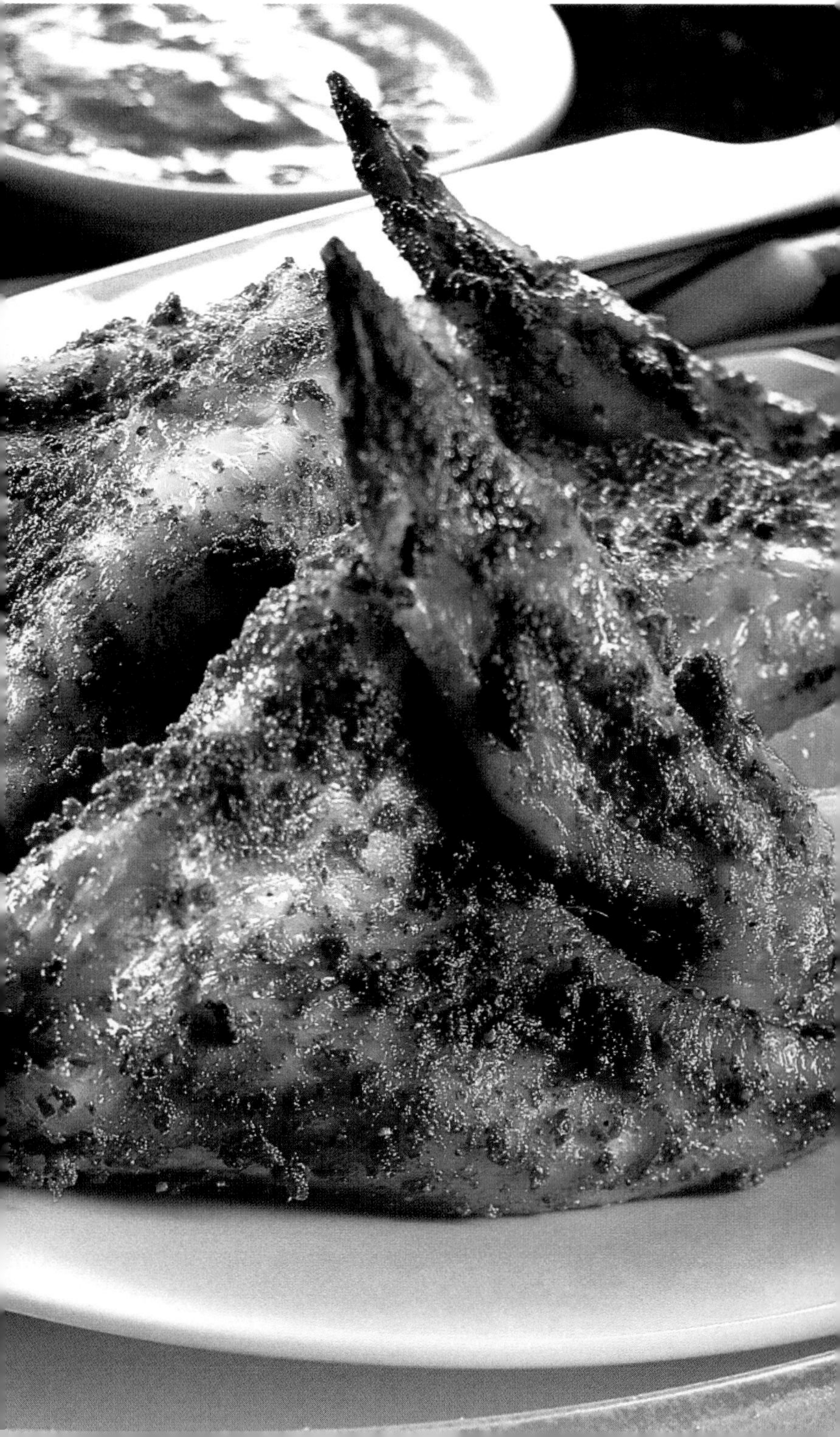

crisp
curried wings

■■□ | Cooking time: 70 minutes - Preparation time: 30 minutes

method

1. Rinse the chicken wings and pat dry with kitchen paper. Rub the curry paste well onto the chicken wings with your fingers, covering all surfaces. Pin back the wing tip to form a triangle. Place in single layer on a tray; stand for 30 minutes in refrigerator, uncovered.

2. Meanwhile place the rice in a 8 cup/2 lt/ 70 fl oz casserole dish; add salt and boiling water. Cover with lid or foil and place on lower shelf oven, preheated at 180°C/350°F/Gas 4. Cook for 40 minutes. Remove from oven and stand, covered, 5 minutes.

3. Transfer chicken wings to a wire rack placed over a baking tray. Place on top shelf of oven above the rice. Cook for 20 minutes, turning once. When rice has been removed, increase oven temperature to 200°C/400°F/Gas 6 for 5 minutes to crisp the wings.

4. Halve the tomatoes and remove the seeds then cut into small dice. Peel cucumber; slice in half lengthwise, remove the seeds with a teaspoon. Dice the cucumber and mix with the diced tomato. Place in a suitable dish, place chutney in a similar dish. Serve the crisp curried wings with the rice and accompanying sambals.

ingredients

> 1 kg/2 lb chicken wings
> 2 tablespoons mild curry paste
> 1¹/2 cups/330 g/11 oz basmati rice, rinsed
> ¹/2 teaspoon salt
> 3 cups/750 ml/1¹/4 pt boiling water
> 2 tomatoes, blanched and skinned
> 1 small cucumber
> 1 cup/240 g/8 oz fruit chutney

tip from the chef

Co-ordinate the cooking so that rice and chicken utilize the same oven.

Serves 4-6

chicken
with spinach filling

■■□ | Cooking time: 44 minutes - Preparation time: 15 minutes

method

1. To make filling, squeeze spinach (a) to remove excess liquid. Place spinach, garlic, ricotta or cottage cheese, Parmesan cheese, lemon rind and nutmeg in a bowl and mix to combine.
2. Using your fingers, loosen skin on chicken (b), starting at thigh end.
3. Push filling gently under skin down into the drumstick (c). Arrange chicken pieces in an ovenproof dish, brush with melted butter and bake at 180°C/350°F/Gas 4 for 35-40 minutes.
4. To make sauce, place tomato purée and Worcestershire sauce in a saucepan, bring to simmering and simmer for 3-4 minutes. Serve sauce with chicken.

....
Serves 4

ingredients

> 4 chicken marylands (uncut leg and thigh joints)
> 30 g/1 oz butter, melted

spinach filling

> 125 g/4 oz frozen spinach, thawed
> 1 clove garlic, crushed
> 125 g/4 oz ricotta or cottage cheese, drained
> 2 teaspoons grated Parmesan cheese
> 1 teaspoon finely grated lemon rind
> pinch ground nutmeg

tomato sauce

> 310 g/10 oz canned tomato purée
> 2 teaspoons Worcestershire sauce

tip from the chef

Drumsticks can be used in place of the chicken marylands. Frozen chicken should be completely thawed before cooking. Thaw birds in refrigerator for 24-36 hours or in microwave on Defrost (30%) for 10-15 minutes per 500 g/1 lb of chicken. Rinse cavity of chicken under cold running water to ensure that there are no remaining ice crystals.

chicken
galantine slices

■ ■ □ | Cooking time: 45 minutes - Preparation time: 35 minutes

method

1. To make filling, place chicken and sausage minces, onion, parsley, garlic, egg and black pepper to taste in a bowl and mix to combine.
2. Place each chicken breast fillet, cut side up, on a flat surface between sheets of plastic food wrap and pound lightly to make a flattened rectangle. Lay 3 slices prosciutto or ham over each rectangle. Place one-sixth of the filling lengthwise down the center, top with a row of 5 prunes and cover with another one-sixth of the filling.
3. Wrap fillets around filling to enclose and tie at 2 cm/3/4 in intervals with kitchen string. Wrap rolls in light buttered aluminum foil and place in a baking dish.
4. Bake at 180°C/350°F/Gas 4 for 30 minutes, remove rolls from foil and bake for 15 minutes or until chicken is cooked. Wrap rolls in clean aluminum foil and refrigerate for several hours or until cold. To serve, remove string and cut into 1 cm/1/2 in thick slices.

ingredients

> **3 double boneless chicken breast fillets**
> **9 slices prosciutto or lean ham**
> **15 pitted dessert prunes**

savory filling

> **375 g/12 oz chicken mince**
> **200 g/6 1/2 oz sausage mince**
> **1 onion, finely chopped**
> **3-4 tablespoons chopped fresh parsley**
> **2 cloves garlic, crushed**
> **1 egg, lightly beaten**
> **freshly ground black pepper**

Makes about 45

tip from the chef

This dish can make for a magnificent starter or for a complete summertime meal, next to a salad.

chicken
and fresh herb terrine

■ ■ □ | Cooking time: 125 minutes - Preparation time: 40 minutes

ingredients

> 1 bunch/500 g/1 lb spinach or silverbeet
> 250 g/8 oz chicken livers, cleaned
> 1 tablespoon seasoned flour
> 15 g/1 oz butter
> 1 teaspoon olive oil
> 375 g/12 oz chicken meat, a mixture of white and dark meat, ground
> 375 g/12 oz lean pork, ground
> 2 teaspoons finely chopped fresh thyme or 1 teaspoon dried thyme
> 3 cloves garlic, crushed
> 2 onions, diced
> 1 tablespoon green peppercorns in brine, drained
> 3 eggs
> 1/2 cup/125 ml/4 fl oz dry white wine
> 2 tablespoons port or sherry
> 3 tablespoons chopped fresh parsley
> freshly ground black pepper

method

1. Preheat oven. Boil, steam or microwave spinach or silverbeet leaves to soften. Drain; refresh under cold running water and drain again. Line a lightly greased terrine dish or an 11 x 21 cm/4 1/2 x 8 1/2 in loaf tin with overlapping spinach leaves. Allow leaves to overhang the sides.

2. Toss chicken livers in seasoned flour to coat. Heat butter and oil in a frying pan over a medium heat until foaming. Add chicken livers and cook, stirring, for 3-5 minutes or until they just change color. Remove livers from pan and set aside to cool.

3. Chop chicken livers. Place chicken livers, chicken, pork, thyme, garlic, onions, green peppercorns, eggs, wine, port or sherry, parsley and black pepper to taste in a bowl and mix to combine.

4. Pack meat mixture into prepared terrine dish or loaf tin, fold overhanging spinach leaves over filling and cover with aluminum foil. Place terrine dish of loaf in a baking dish with enough boiling water to come halfway up the sides of the dish and bake at 180°C/350°F/Gas 4 for 2 hours. Drain off juices, cover top of terrine with foil, then weight and set aside to cool. When cold, refrigerate overnight. To serve, unmold and cut into slices.

....
Serves 10

crusty
chicken goulash

■□□ | Cooking time: 60 minutes - Preparation time: 10 minutes

method

1. Heat 1 tablespoon oil in a large frying pan and cook onions, stirring, over a medium heat for 5-6 minutes or until golden. Remove onions from pan and set aside. Combine paprika and flour in a plastic food bag, add chicken, shake to coat with flour mixture, then shake off excess flour mixture.

2. Heat remaining oil in frying pan and cook chicken, stirring, over a medium heat for 2-3 minutes. Return onions to pan, stir in tomato paste (purée), wine and stock. Bring to the boil, stirring constantly, then reduce heat, cover and simmer for 6-7 minutes. Remove from heat, stir in yogurt and cool.

3. To make crust, place butter, sour cream and egg in a bowl. Stir in flour and parsley and mix well to combine (a).

4. To assemble, place crust mixture in an 8 cup/2 liter/3½ pt lightly greased casserole dish and work mixture to cover sides and base of dish (b).

5. Spoon filling into crust (c), cover with lid of dish and bake at 180°C/350°F/Gas 4 for 35 minutes. Remove lid and bake for 10 minutes longer.

ingredients

> 2 tablespoons vegetable oil
> 2 large onions, chopped
> 1½ tablespoons paprika
> 2 tablespoons seasoned flour
> 500 g/1 lb boneless chicken breast fillets, cut into strips
> 1 tablespoon tomato paste (purée)
> ½ cup/125 ml/4 fl oz red wine
> ½ cup/125 ml/4 fl oz chicken stock
> 3 tablespoons natural yogurt

sour cream crust

> 125 g/4 oz butter, softened
> 300 g/9½ oz sour cream
> 1 egg
> 1 cup/125 g/4 oz self-raising flour, sifted
> 1 tablespoon chopped fresh parsley

Serves 4

tip from the chef

A chicken goulash surrounded by a rich sour cream crust is just the thing for that special occasion. Serve this delicious chicken with a tossed green salad or boiled, steamed or microwaved green vegetables such as green beans, zucchini, snow peas or asparagus.

chicken
with garlic and pepper

■ □ □ | Cooking time: 5 minutes - Preparation time: 10 minutes

ingredients
> **4 cloves garlic**
> **3 fresh coriander roots**
> **1 teaspoon crushed black peppercorns**
> **500 g/1 lb chicken breast fillets, chopped into 3 cm/1 1/4 in cubes**
> **vegetable oil for deep-frying**
> **30 g/1 oz fresh basil leaves**
> **30 g/1 oz fresh mint leaves**
> **sweet chili sauce**

method
1. Place garlic, coriander roots and black peppercorns in a food processor and process to make a paste. Coat chicken with garlic paste and marinate for 1 hour.
2. Heat oil in a wok or frying pan over a high heat until a cube of bread dropped in browns in 50 seconds, then deep-fry chicken, a few pieces at a time, for 2 minutes or until golden and tender. Drain on absorbent kitchen paper.
3. Deep-fry basil and mint until crisp, then drain and place on a serving plate. Top with chicken and serve with chili sauce.

....
Serves 4

tip from the chef
Thai cooks use three types of basil in cooking –Asian sweet, holy and lemon – each has a distinctive flavor and is used for specific types of dishes. For this dish, Asian sweet basil, known in Thailand as horapa, would be used.

southern-fried
chicken drumsticks

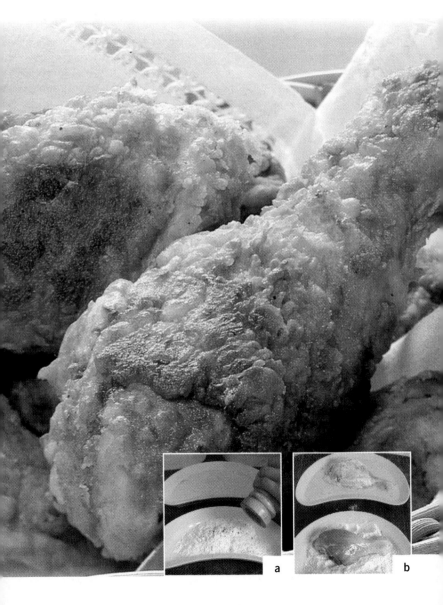

a

b

■ □ □ I Cooking time: 35 minutes - Preparation time: 10 minutes

method

1. Rinse drumsticks and pat dry with paper towel. Smooth skin over the drumsticks.
2. Mix flour, salt and pepper (a), place on paper-lined, flat plate. Beat eggs and milk well together in a deep plate.
3. Dip the drumsticks in the flour (b) then into the egg, turning to coat both sides. Place again in the flour, lift end of paper to toss flour over drumstick and roll in flour until well covered. Place in single layer on a clean, flat tray.
4. Heat oil in a large frying pan. Add drumsticks and fry a few minutes on each side (c) until just beginning to color. Reduce heat, place a lid on the pan and cook slowly for 20 minutes, turning chicken after 10 minutes (d).
5. Remove lid and increase heat, continue cooking until golden brown and crisp, turning frequently. Remove from pan, drain on paper towels (e). Serve hot with vegetable accompaniments.

ingredients

> 1 kg/2 lb chicken drumsticks
> 1¹/2 cups/180 g/6 fl oz flour
> 1 teaspoon salt and pepper
> 2 eggs
> ¹/3 cup/80 ml/3 fl oz milk
> ¹/2 cup/120 ml/4 fl oz canola oil

tip from the chef

Pan-fried chicken is a temptation for grown-ups and children alike. It goes fantastic with a three color mash (potato, pumpkin and spinach).

Serves 4

c

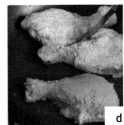

d

e

chicken
with lime and coconut

■□□ | Cooking time: 20 minutes - Preparation time: 10 minutes

ingredients

> 1 kg/2 lb chicken thigh or breast fillets, cut into thick strips
> 1 tablespoon Thai red curry paste
> 1 tablespoon vegetable oil
> 3 tablespoons palm or brown sugar
> 4 kaffir lime leaves
> 2 teaspoons finely grated lime rind
> 1 cup/250 ml/8 fl oz coconut cream
> 1 tablespoon Thai fish sauce (nam pla)
> 2 tablespoons coconut vinegar
> 3 tablespoons shredded coconut
> 4 fresh red chilies, sliced

method

1. Place chicken and curry paste in a bowl and toss to coat. Heat oil in a wok or large saucepan over a high heat, add chicken and stir-fry for 4-5 minutes or until lightly browned and fragrant.

2. Add sugar, lime leaves, lime rind, coconut cream and fish sauce and cook, stirring, over a medium heat for 3-4 minutes or until the sugar dissolves and caramelizes.

3. Stir in vinegar and coconut and simmer until chicken is tender. Serve with chilies in a dish on the side.

....
Serves 4

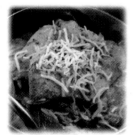

tip from the chef

For something a little different, serve this dish with egg noodles.

sweet chicken
drumsticks with

char-grilled
tarragon chicken

method

1. Place chicken in a single layer in a shallow glass or ceramic dish. Combine tarragon, wine, lemon rind and green peppercorns. Pour marinade over chicken. Turn to coat chicken with marinade and marinate at room temperature, turning once, for 20 minutes.

2. Remove chicken from marinade and cook on a preheated hot char grill or in a preheated grill pan for 5 minutes or until tender.

ingredients

> 6 boneless chicken breast fillets, skin removed
> 3 tablespoons chopped fresh tarragon or 2 teaspoons dried tarragon
> 1 cup/250 ml/8 fl oz dry white wine
> 2 tablespoons lemon rind strips
> 1 tablespoon green peppercorns in brine, drained and crushed

....

Serves 6

tip from the chef

Do not marinate chicken any longer than 20 minutes as the marinade will cause the chicken to break down.

spicy
mango chicken

■■□ | Cooking time: 10 minutes - Preparation time: 40 minutes

method

1. Preheat barbecue to a high heat. Place chicken between sheets of greaseproof paper and pound lightly with a meat mallet to flatten to 1 cm/1/2 in thick.

2. Combine black pepper, cumin and paprika and sprinkle over chicken. Layer prosciutto or ham and mango slices on chicken, roll up and secure with wooden toothpicks or cocktail sticks. Place chicken on lightly oiled barbecue and cook for 3-5 minutes each side or until chicken is tender and cooked.

3. To make sauce, place mango, garlic, golden syrup and chili sauce in a small saucepan and cook, stirring, over a low heat for 4-5 minutes or until sauce thickens slightly. Serve with chicken.

Serves 4

ingredients

> **4 boneless chicken breast fillets**
> **1 teaspoon freshly ground black pepper**
> **1 teaspoon ground cumin**
> **1 teaspoon paprika**
> **4 slices prosciutto or ham, halved**
> **2 mangoes, peeled and cut into 2 cm/3/4 in thick slices**

mango sauce

> **1 mango, peeled and chopped**
> **1 clove garlic, crushed**
> **2 tablespoons golden syrup**
> **1 tablespoon sweet chili sauce**

tip from the chef

Drained, canned mangoes can be used in place of fresh. You will need two 440 g/14 oz cans of mangoes. Use three-quarters of one can for the sauce and the remainder for the filling in the chicken.

teriyaki
tenderloins

■ □ □ | Cooking time: 5 minutes - Preparation time: 5 minutes

method

1. Place tenderloins in a non-metal container and stir in about 3/4 cup Teriyaki marinade. Cover and marinate for 30 minutes at room temperature or several hours or overnight in the refrigerator.

2. Heat the barbecue until hot. Place a sheet of baking paper over the grill bars and make a few slits between the bars for ventilation, or place baking paper on the hot plate. Place the tenderloins on grill and cook for 2 minutes on each side until cooked through and golden. Brush with marinade as they cook. Serve immediately with extra Teriyaki marinade as a dipping sauce.

Serves 4

ingredients

> **500 g/1 lb chicken tenderloins**
> **375 g/12 1/2 oz bottle Teriyaki marinade**

tip from the chef

Serving suggestions
- *Serve with steamed rice and vegetables.*
- *Toss into salad greens to make a hot salad. Dress salad with 1 tablespoon Teriyaki marinade, 1 tablespoon vinegar and 3 tablespoons salad oil.*
- *Stuff into heated pocket breads along with shredded lettuce, cucumber and onion rings and drizzle with an extra spoonful of Teriyaki marinade.*

index